ADVENTURES OF CELERINA

Interactive Journal

Myriah Mathews

www.alour-artist.com

© 2022 Myriah Mathews

Second Edition

Printed with: Ingramsparks

ISBN: 979-8-9871513-3-4 (Print)

Edited by: Debbie Dunn

This journal is designed for you to color, reflect,
and explore wherever each drawing takes you.
Write about the emotions that arise, what you
are grateful for, positive affirmations, or the
moments that shape your day.

As you move through these pages, you may uncover
pieces of yourself that invite healing or highlight
the many positive ways you already live.
Your discoveries may surprise and inspire you.

You are welcome to add extra pages anytime.

I am releasing the fear of what I want most
so I am open to receive what I want.

With appreciation to my dog Beau, my parents
Debbie and Camron, and the friends and clients
who continue to encourage and support me.

Oregon

Positive affirmations used daily is life altering.
Throughout this journal there will be places for you to
write your gratitude and positive statements.
Feel fee to use a separate sheet of paper if needed.

Celerina

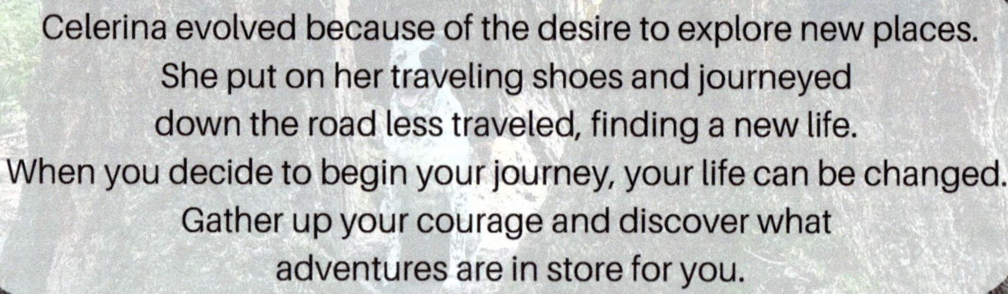
Celerina evolved because of the desire to explore new places.
She put on her traveling shoes and journeyed
down the road less traveled, finding a new life.
When you decide to begin your journey, your life can be changed.
Gather up your courage and discover what
adventures are in store for you.

What do you wish to find out about yourself?
What adventures do you want to explore?
What is one thing you want to change in your life?
Do you believe you can have anything you desire?

McMinnville, Oregon

What are you grateful for?
(I am grateful for my health, I am grateful for my loving family.)
Listen to your heart, there is so much to be thankful for.
Even if at times this may feel challenging, once you
get started it becomes easier to find more
things in which to be grateful.

Story Teller

The stories we tell ourselves shape our present and future.
The story teller shares both positive and negative
affirmations, and it effects her face and body.
(I am beautiful, I am strong, I am worthy, etc.)
The negative ones can split your world like a lighting bolt.
The pathway to positive thinking can be transformative.

What happened today? What came up for you?
Use the space below to write what you've
discovered or uncovered about yourself?

Ketchum, Idaho

Is hiking your thing? Biking? Fishing? Dinning out?
If so, Ketchum is a beautiful place to visit.

Statements in the present tense help the mind bring what
you ask into your life. (I am, I have, I feel happy and radiant.)

"When you learn to nurture and love yourself as you
would another, when you give yourself that
attention, things change very fast.
Things move in you." Lee Harris

10

Nan is here to remind us of the joys of vacation, of traveling and exploring the world around us. Taking time away from work is some of the best medicine. It helps give perspective and a fresh outlook on life. Take the time, you deserve it.

What was your favorite vacation?
What is a place you would like to go visit?
What steps are required for you to go on that vacation?
Are the steps something you are willing to take
so you can go exploring?

The Creatures of the Land

Tips for effective affirmations:
*Be specific - Clearly define what you wish to receive or be.
*Hear the sounds in that vision.
*See vibrantly your surroundings.
*Feel yourself already having it or being what you want to be.
*Feel joy and excitement for being there.
*Give thanks for being able to hear, see, feel and know
deep in the well of you. You deserve what you seek.
*Then release the attachments to a time frame and the outcome.
*Go about your day knowing you've done what you can.

Spiritwalker

Spiritwalker reminds us the answers we seek are all around.
Each creature has its own message to give. Next time a bird
flies in front of you or a frog jumps across your path,
listen with your heart to hear what they may have to say.

Wanting clarity? Have you been asking for guidance?
Praying to know where to go to next?
Asking your question is the first step to receive the answers.
Listening is the second step.

Lost in Idaho

What activities bring you joy? Do you put on music and
dance around? Practice yoga? Take a walk in nature?
Meet up with loved ones? Go for a bike ride?
Make a yummy meal?
When one lives in a state of joy each moment flows freely.

Be patient with yourself if gratitude statements,
and positive affirmations are new for you.
It takes time to reprogram old thoughts into new habits.
If you are familiar to these ways of thinking yet have
forgotten the benefits of them, not to worry life gets hectic
at times. Start again with love and gratitude for yourself
for remembering.

Time Traveler

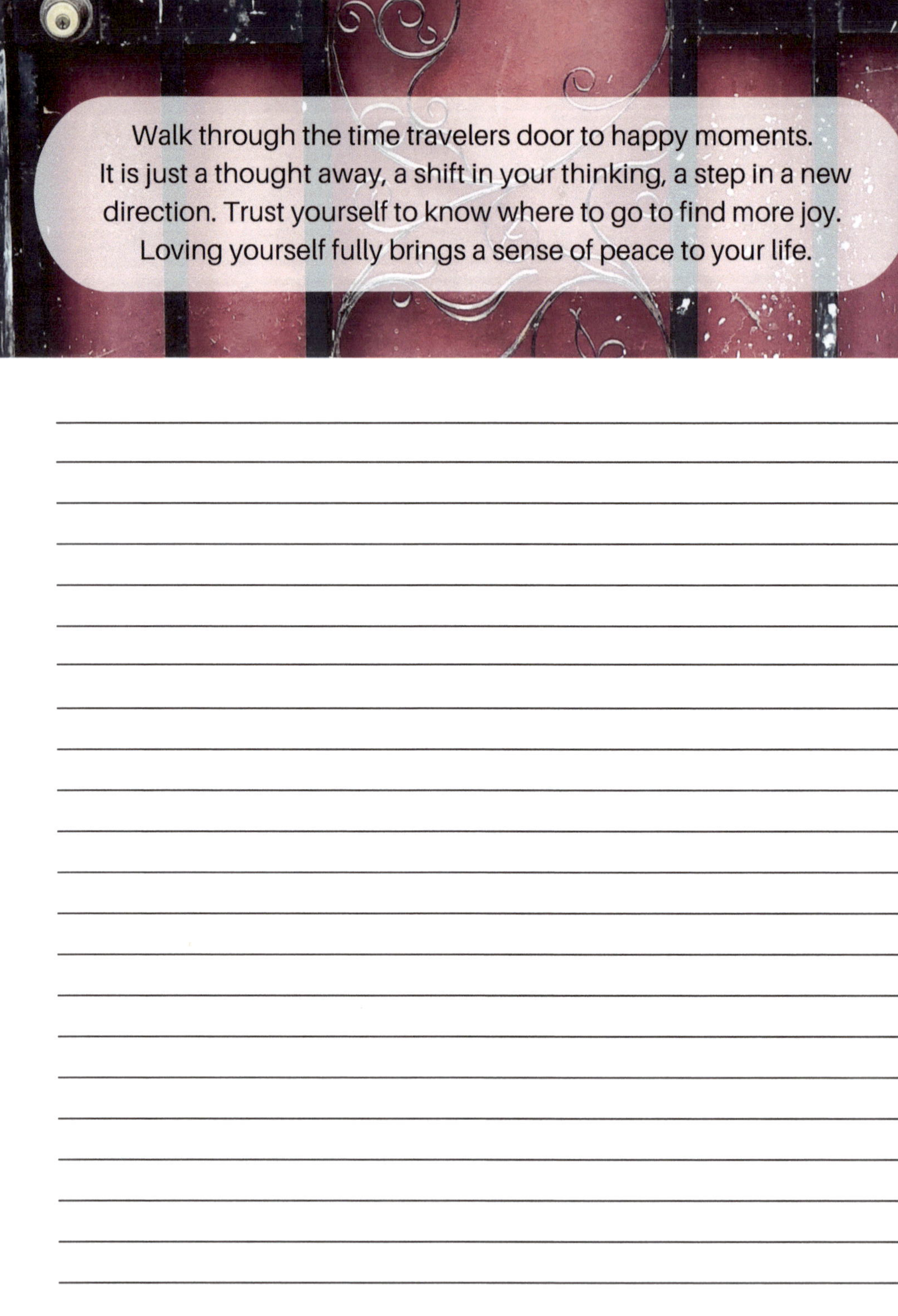

Walk through the time travelers door to happy moments.
It is just a thought away, a shift in your thinking, a step in a new direction. Trust yourself to know where to go to find more joy.
Loving yourself fully brings a sense of peace to your life.

Dreaming of another land? Another time, when you
felt alive and free to jump as high as you could?
Write below the places that bring you joy.
What did you do today to embrace your happiness?

Colorado

Jerome Arizona

Did you find yourself saying positive statements today?
If so what were they?
What happenings created a sense of gratitude for you?
(I am grateful I am taking the time to play,
I am blessed for all those who play in life with me.)

Child Within

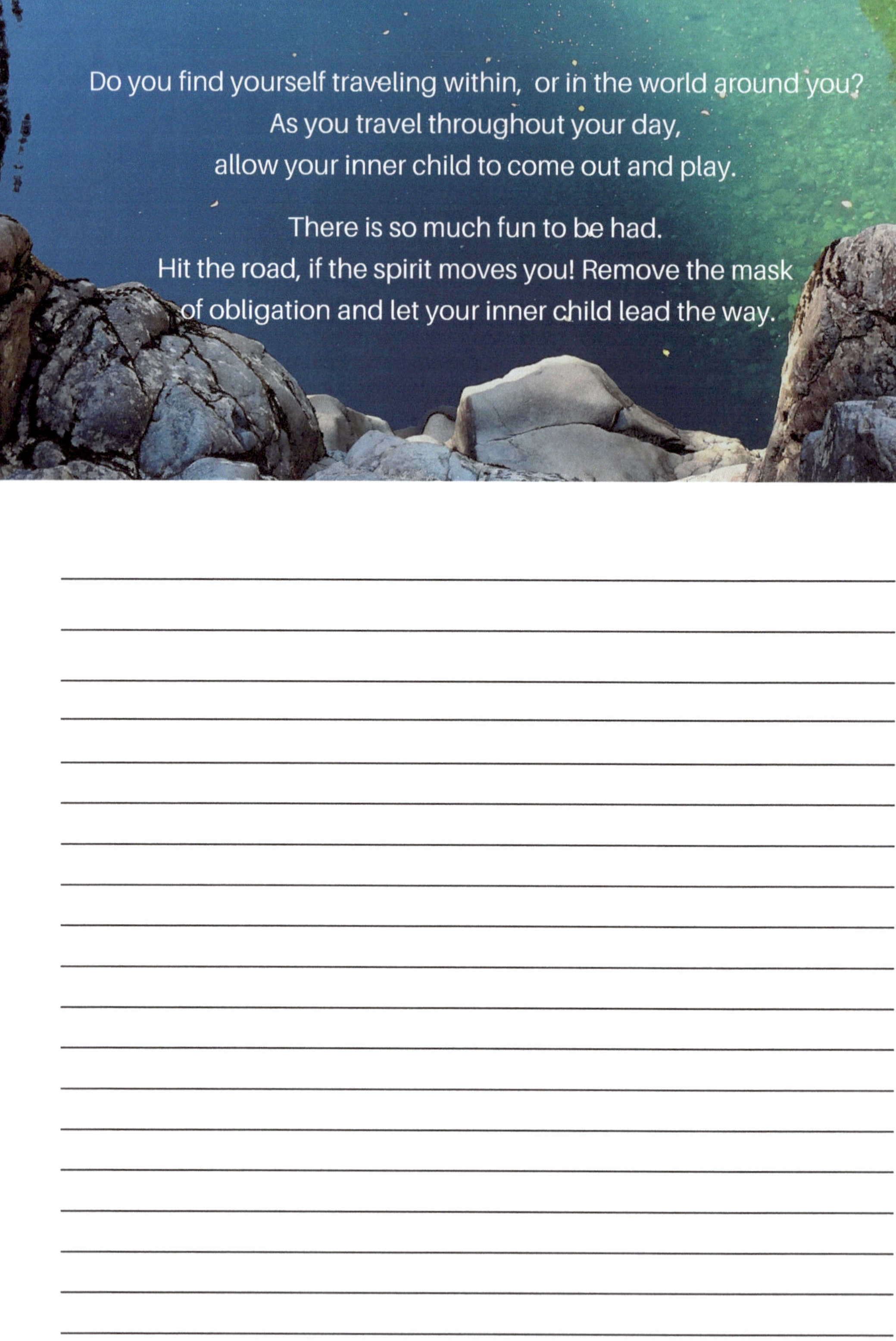

Do you find yourself traveling within, or in the world around you?
As you travel throughout your day,
allow your inner child to come out and play.

There is so much fun to be had.
Hit the road, if the spirit moves you! Remove the mask
of obligation and let your inner child lead the way.

What is the first thing you noticed about the image?
How did it make your feel?
What is your inner child wanting to share with you?

Drift Creek Falls, Oregon   Redwoods, Califorina

What brought you joy and happiness today?
May blessings of many kinds find their way to you.
Send some positivity to others and allow
positivity to flow back to you multiplied.

Roche Harbor Resort, Washington

Inner Jungle

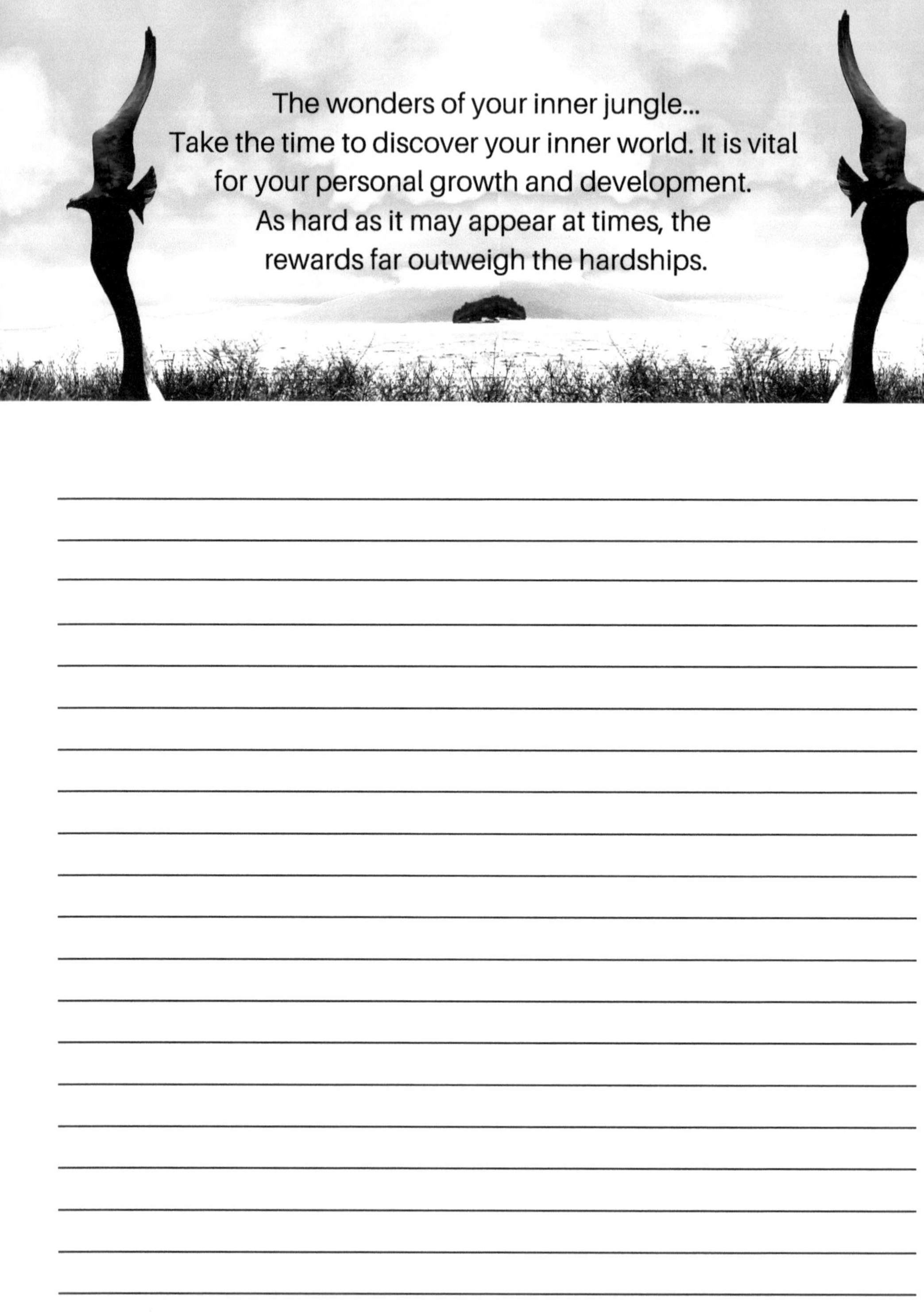
The wonders of your inner jungle...
Take the time to discover your inner world. It is vital
for your personal growth and development.
As hard as it may appear at times, the
rewards far outweigh the hardships.

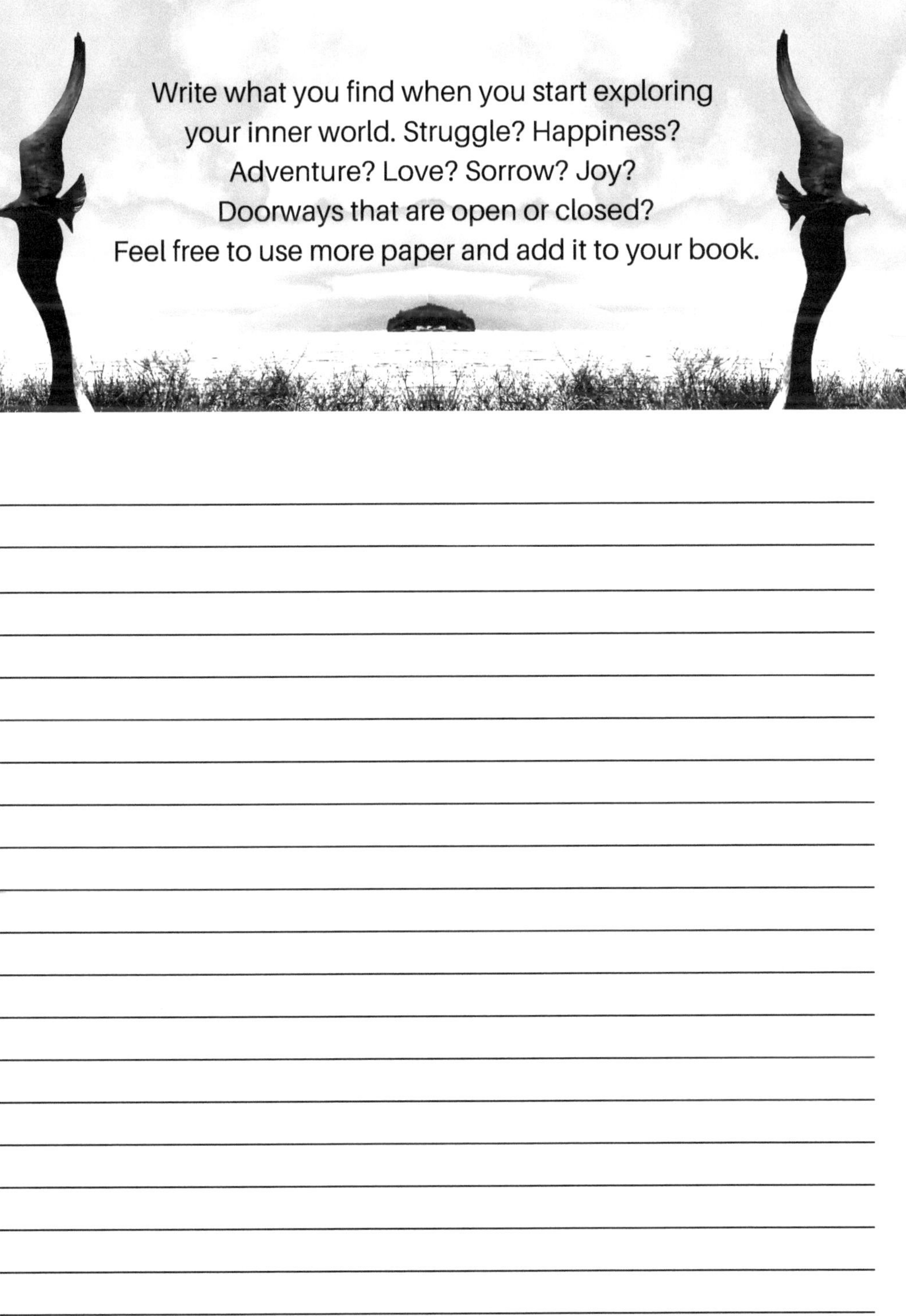

Write what you find when you start exploring
your inner world. Struggle? Happiness?
Adventure? Love? Sorrow? Joy?
Doorways that are open or closed?
Feel free to use more paper and add it to your book.

Beauty of time

Idaho (near Wyoming)

Dayton, Oregon
A favorite place for
my brothers family

New adventures await your arrival. Even if it's trying a new place in your local area. Once there, notice how you feel. Does it make you feel alive? Overwhelmed? Grateful? Did you get to meet new people? What was your favorite moment in your new experience?

Life's Playground

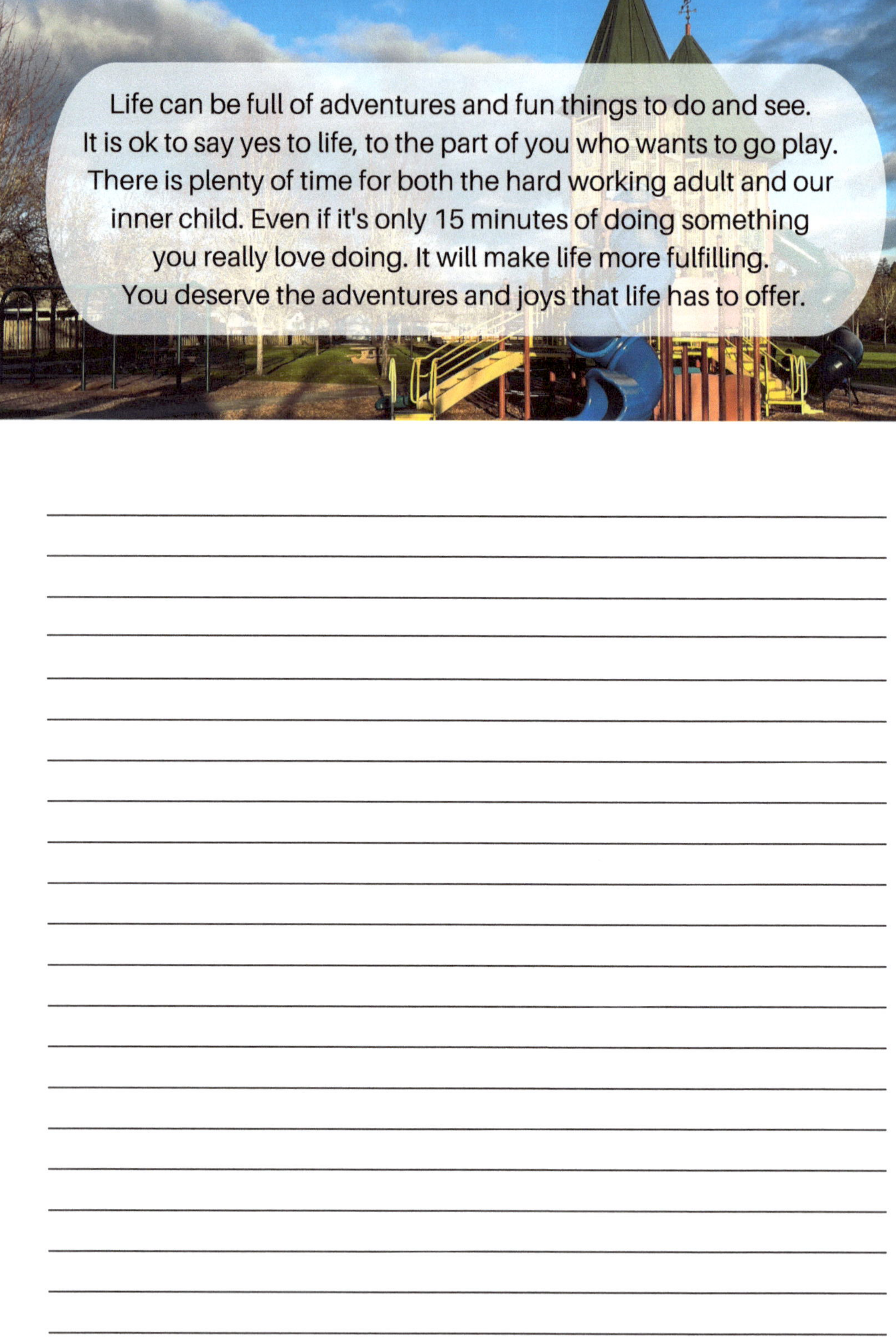

Life can be full of adventures and fun things to do and see.
It is ok to say yes to life, to the part of you who wants to go play.
There is plenty of time for both the hard working adult and our
inner child. Even if it's only 15 minutes of doing something
you really love doing. It will make life more fulfilling.
You deserve the adventures and joys that life has to offer.

Is time feeling broken in your world?
Not feeling like you have enough of it? Wanting more time?
What are you going to do to create more opportunity to play?

Jerome, Arizona

What are ways you can bring more gratitude into your life?
What are some positive affirmations you can say about yourself?

(I have exciting adventures ahead of me.)
(Money flows freely to me in joyous ways.)

Explorer

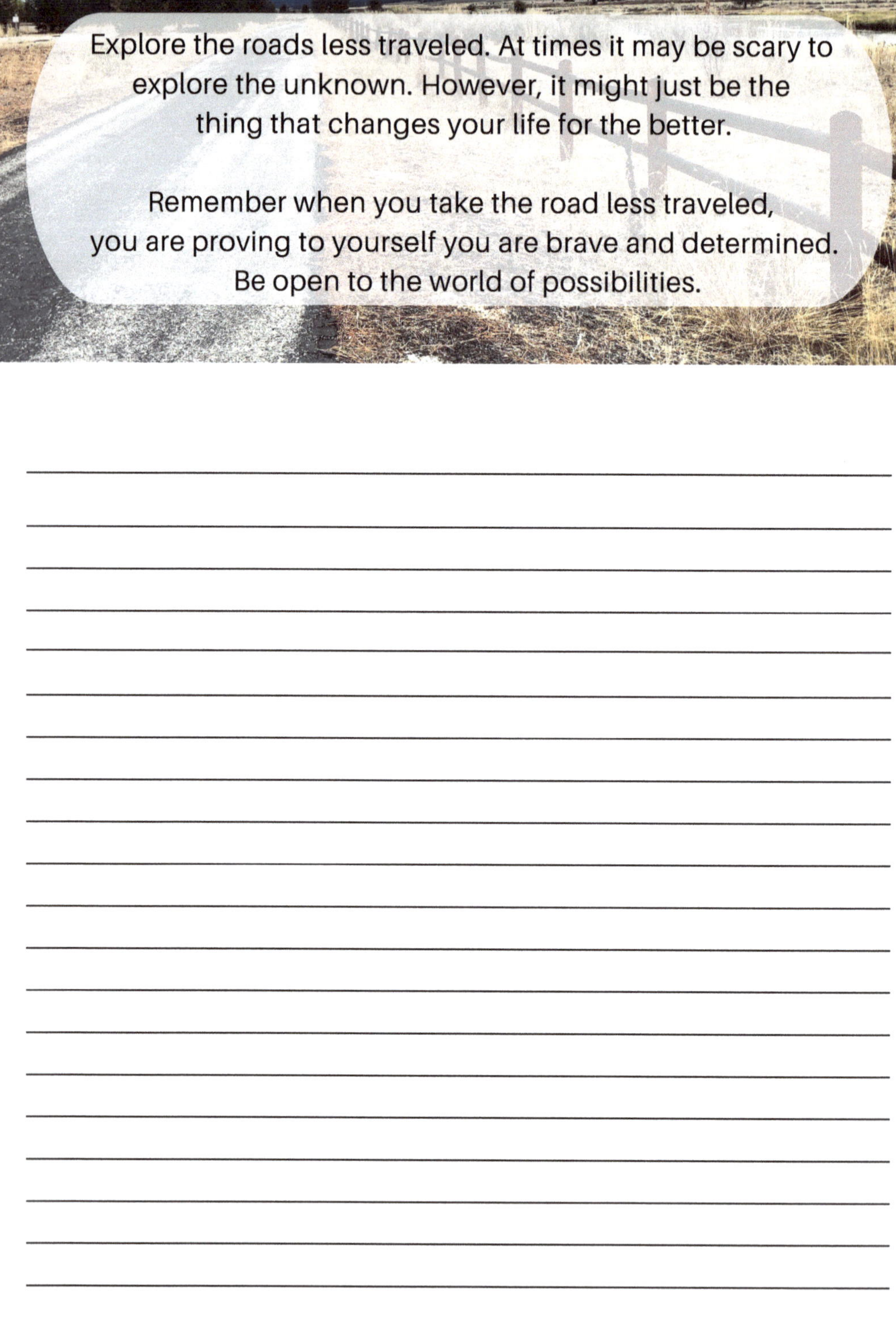

Explore the roads less traveled. At times it may be scary to explore the unknown. However, it might just be the thing that changes your life for the better.

Remember when you take the road less traveled, you are proving to yourself you are brave and determined. Be open to the world of possibilities.

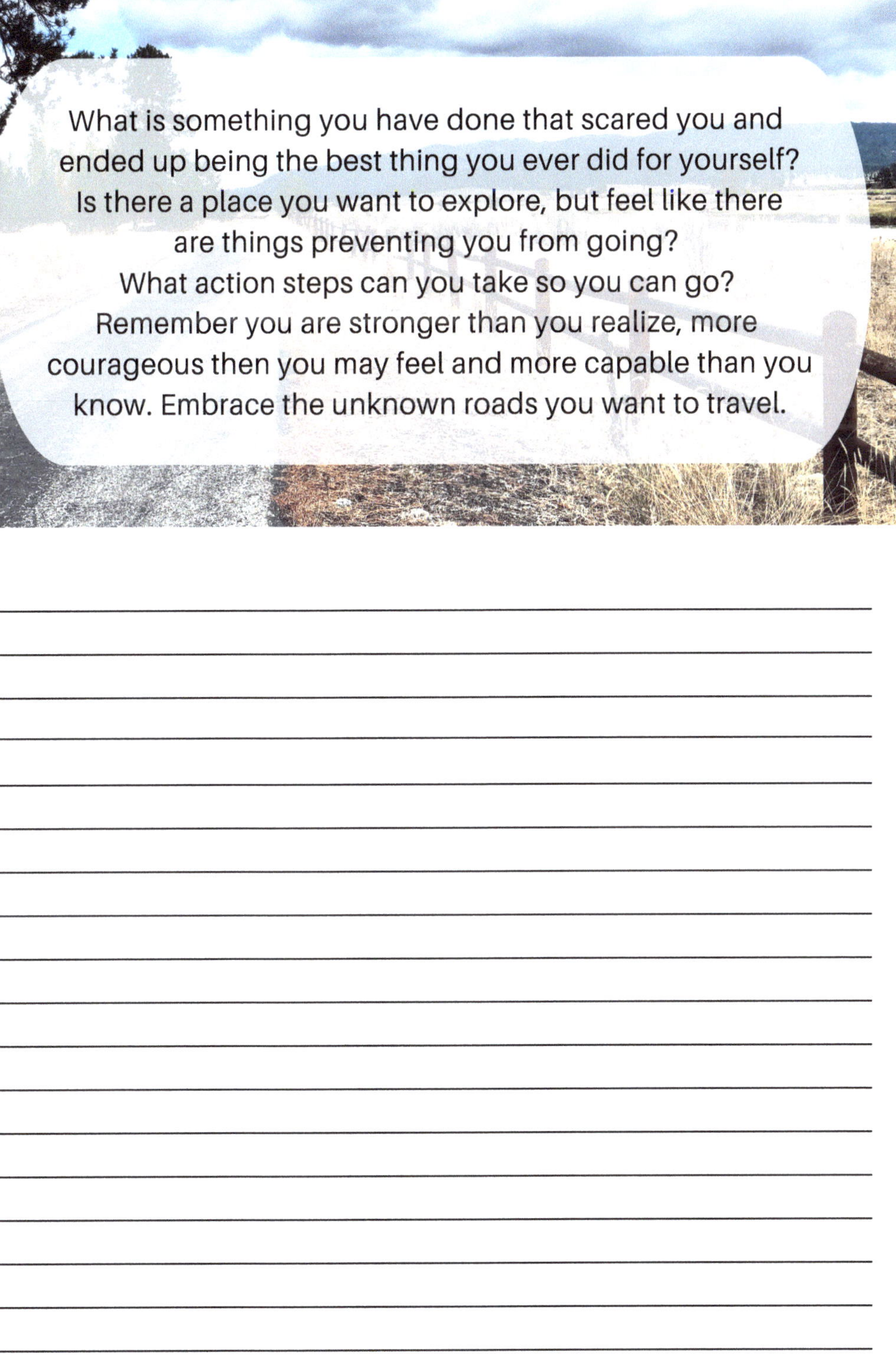

What is something you have done that scared you and
ended up being the best thing you ever did for yourself?
Is there a place you want to explore, but feel like there
are things preventing you from going?
What action steps can you take so you can go?
Remember you are stronger than you realize, more
courageous then you may feel and more capable than you
know. Embrace the unknown roads you want to travel.

Fort Casey State Park, Coupeville, Washington

"Self - approval and self - acceptance in the now moment
are the keys to positive changes in every area of our lives."

Written by: Louise Hay

"I choose to focus on the positive."
"I love and accept myself as I am."
"I attract healthy and loving relationships."

Misty

On the empty road, you can find your way.
Let gentle Misty remind you that your light house can be lit
at any moment. Whether you are lost in confusion or stuck in
despair, the way to illuminate your path resides within you.

What feelings have been coming up for you?
Feeling enlightened? Feeling happy with where you are in life?
No matter what you're feeling in this moment,
acknowledge that it is ok to be there.

Roche Harbor Resort, Washington

The light inside me is shining brighter today, as I have
uncovered and released many things yesterday.

Be at peace, walk with a lightness as you go about your day.
With feeling happy and full of gratitude, send some
to others so they too may feel a sense of ease.

Keeper of the Lighthouse

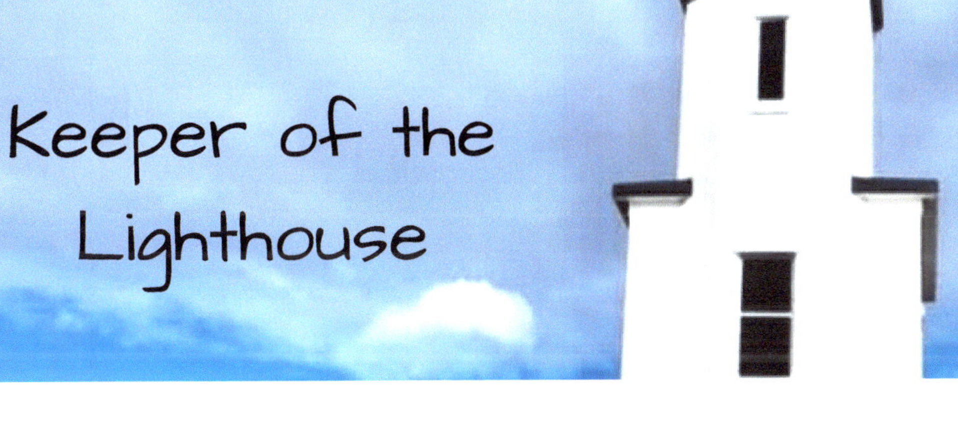

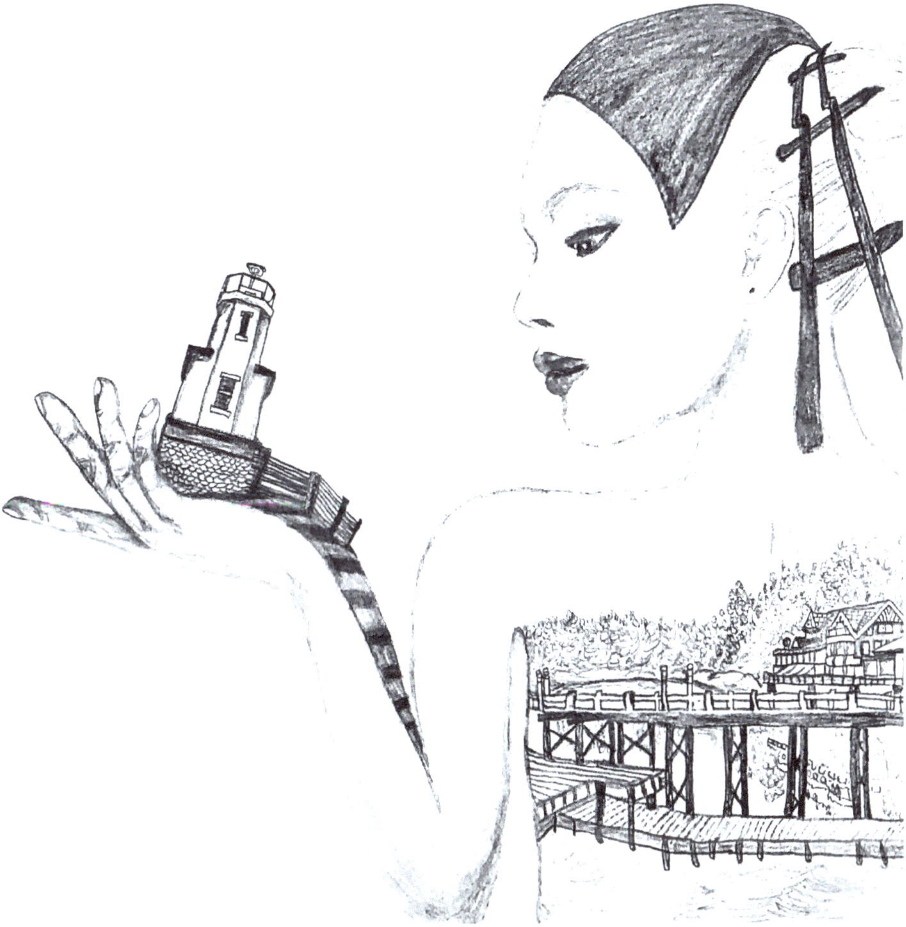

Sometimes it's easier to shine the light for
others then it is for ourselves.
Let the Keeper of the Lighthouse
be your harbor. Offering a beacon through
the fog. She can help guide you to safety.
Once you have landed, walk together
on the path of discovery.

Have you ever felt like you were always helping
others and no one was helping you?
Do you prefer to help others rather than yourself?
Are you feeling you could use some extra light to find your
way to new beginnings? Allow others to shine their light
for you. Remember the light within is bright.

The keeper of the light is guiding you to your light
switch as you make your way through this time.
I am sending you love and light dear one,
for I know what it feels like to walk in the dark.

Lafayette, Colorado

McMinnville, Oregon

I welcome magical moments into my life.
I move beyond old limitations into gratitude.

I have... I am... I believe... I can...
Finish the statements in your mind or on paper

Freckles

Looking within may be the thing you fear the most.
Which means it is also the most rewarding.

What are you not allowing yourself let go of?
What do you fear the most when you are asked to look within?
Place pen to paper and allow words to flow freely with
no judgement. See if the answers come to you.

Portland, Oregon

What passions in your life are you grateful for?
(I am grateful for my creativity, I am thankful for my camera, etc.)

"Passion is energy. Feel the power that comes from
focusing on what excites you." Oprah Winfrey

"Love what you do and what you love. Passion is the
key that opens the door to joy and abundance."
David Cuschieri

Fredrick

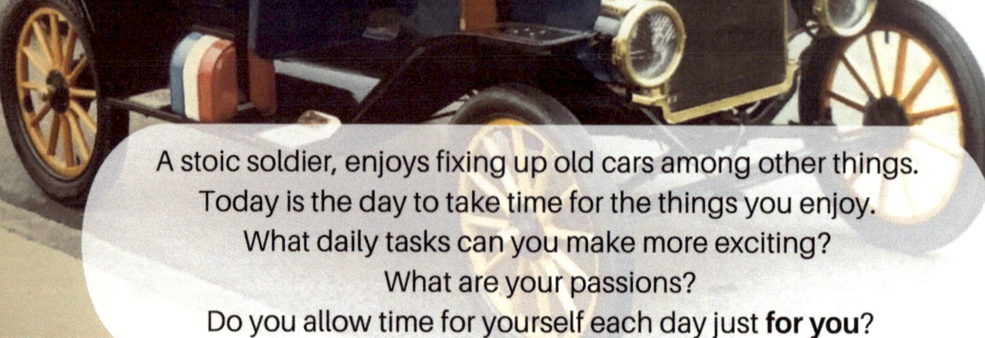

A stoic soldier, enjoys fixing up old cars among other things.
Today is the day to take time for the things you enjoy.
What daily tasks can you make more exciting?
What are your passions?
Do you allow time for yourself each day just **for you**?

Are you stoic like Fredrick, accepting
whatever is happening in your life?
Do you show your emotions for others to see?
Do you bottle up your emotions or let them out in private?
No answer is wrong as it is true for you.

"I trust the process of life."
"Life supports me in every possiable way."
"I am in the right place, at the right time,
doing the right thing for me."
Louise Hay

Which shoes are best for your day?
The shoes we wear are our foundation.
By wearing the right kind shoes for the activity we
choose, sets us up to have a successful day.

Pathways

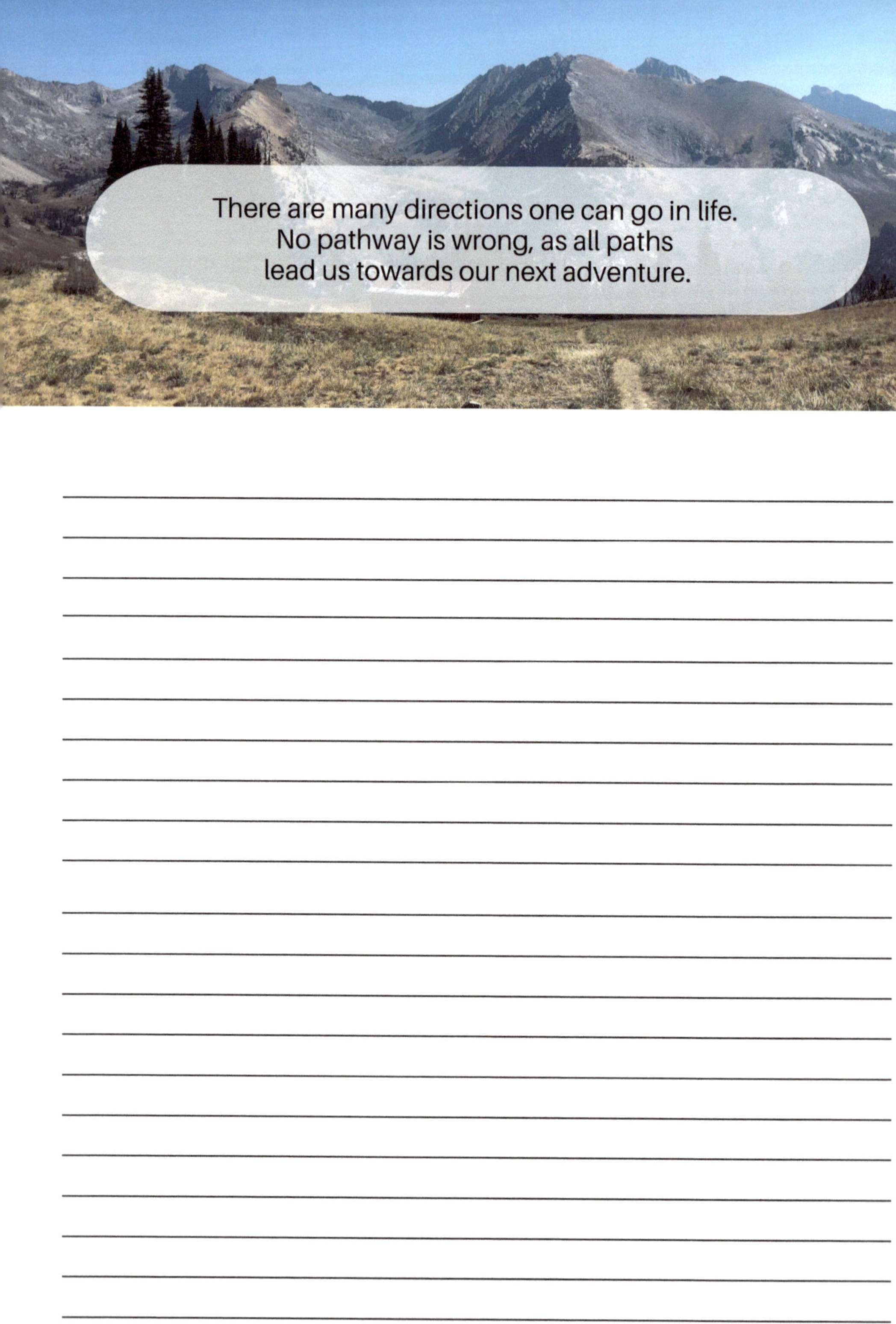
There are many directions one can go in life.
No pathway is wrong, as all paths
lead us towards our next adventure.

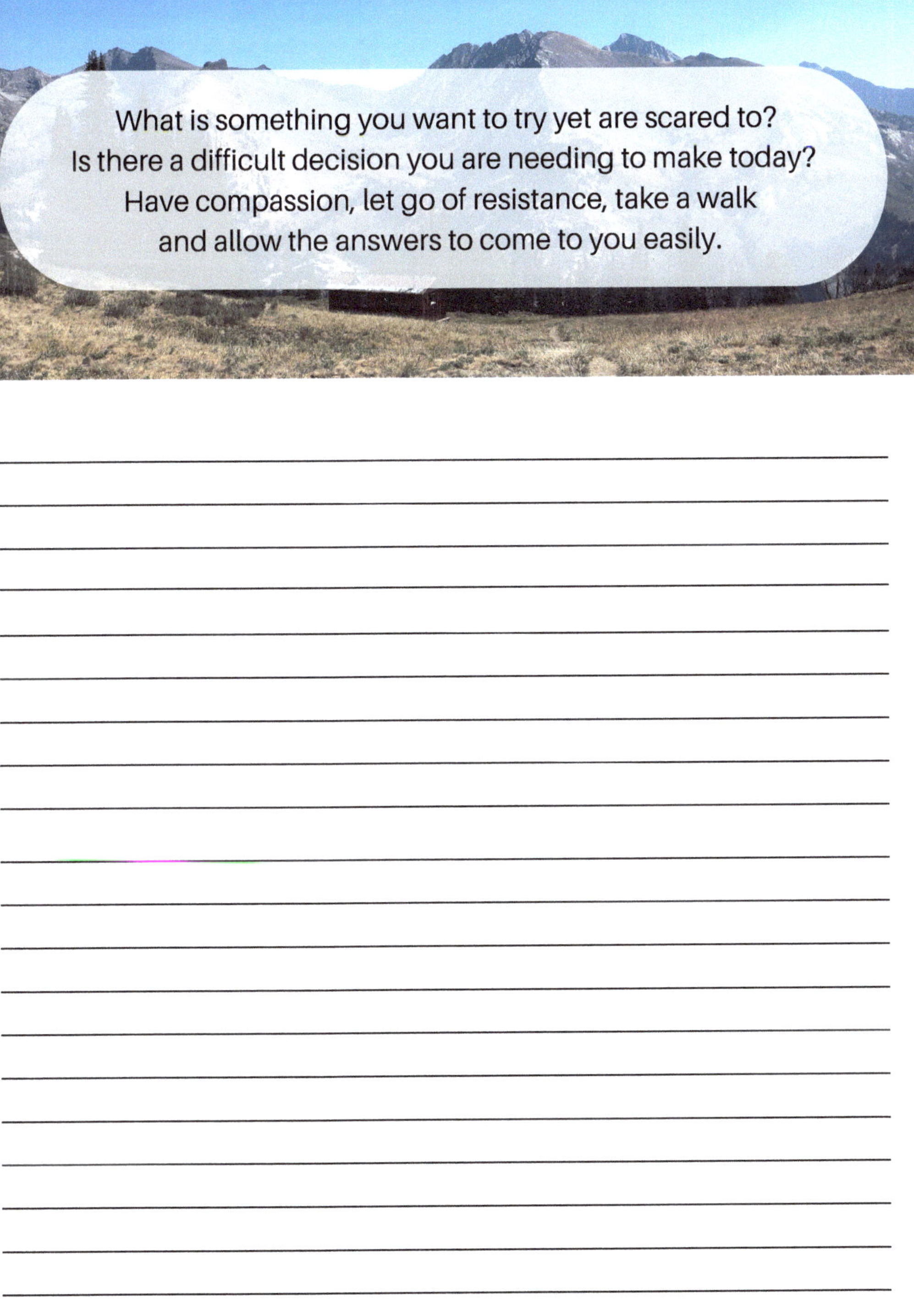

What is something you want to try yet are scared to?
Is there a difficult decision you are needing to make today?
Have compassion, let go of resistance, take a walk
and allow the answers to come to you easily.

Jacksonville, Oregon

After going through your day, what are you grateful for?
What positive beliefs did you tell yourself today?
(I am grateful for the clean air. I am fluidly moving through life.)

Rockell Whispers

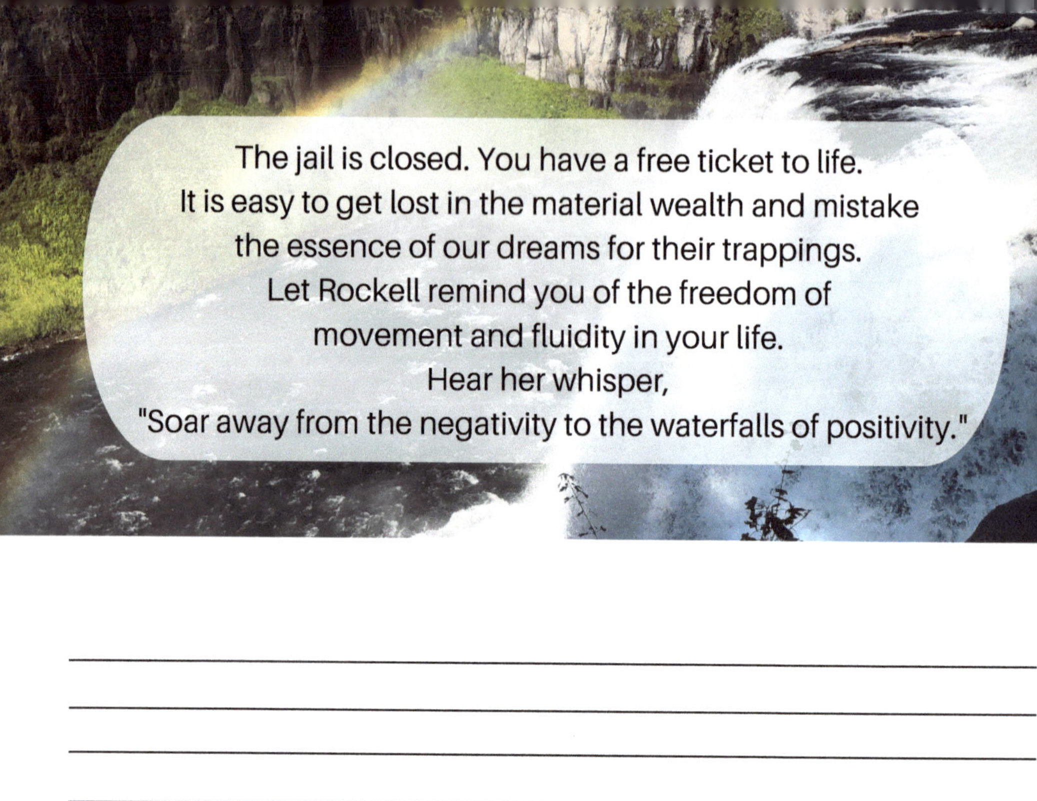

The jail is closed. You have a free ticket to life.
It is easy to get lost in the material wealth and mistake
the essence of our dreams for their trappings.
Let Rockell remind you of the freedom of
movement and fluidity in your life.
Hear her whisper,
"Soar away from the negativity to the waterfalls of positivity."

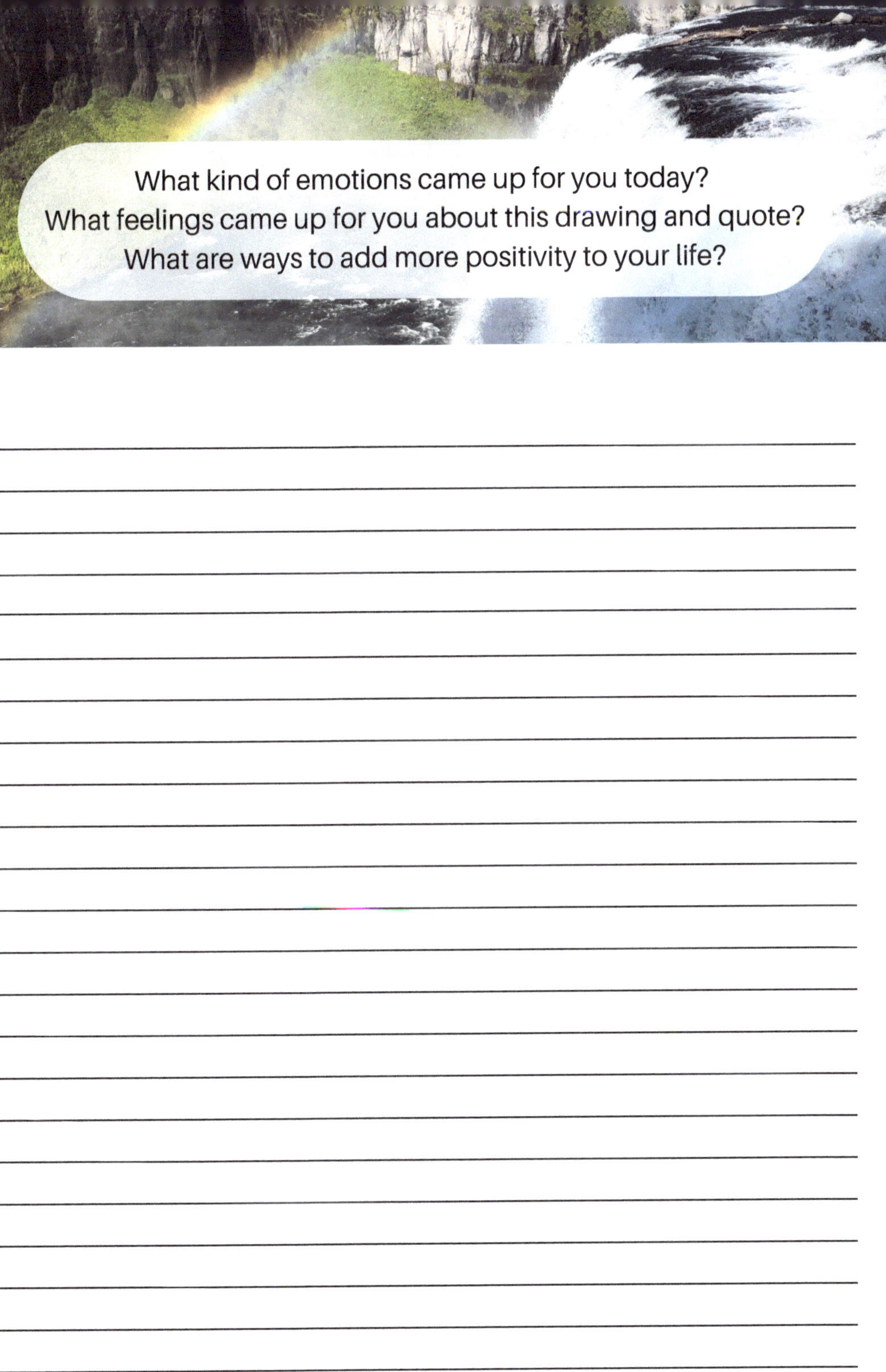

What kind of emotions came up for you today?
What feelings came up for you about this drawing and quote?
What are ways to add more positivity to your life?

Anacortes, Washington

Invoke your inner magic and know you are worthy.
You are important and a treasure to others.
We need you!
We are grateful for your gifts and the time you share.

Angeleen

Angeleen is here to remind us when we release the
burdens, new opportunities present themselves.
The magic of life is all around you, embrace it.

What are ways you can invoke your inner magic?
What joys did you get to embark on today?
What was the happy moment you were excited about?

Ketchum, Idaho

I am embracing positive changes in my life.
I am grateful for my friends who help make life better.
Are you grateful for who you are and where you are?

You are not alone in this journey.
There are plenty of people who
love and care for you.
Surprise those you love by expressing
how grateful you are for them.

Angel

Tied down yet ready to fly?
I am free from the entrapments that have been holding me back.
I am soaring to new heights, exploring new adventures
and letting go of what no longer serves me.
I am free to fly.

Life is ever changing. Take small action steps everyday.
Acceptance of where you are in life, knowing where you want
to go can make a positive impact in your world.
You have what it takes to better your life.
Surround yourself with uplifting people that can help you
on your journey. See a need, fill a need.
Hold open a door for another, volunteer your time.
What you put out so do you receive.

Mount Hood, Oregon

The more you practice self-love, self-care, positive affirmations and gratitude for all you have and all you are, the more you will attract health, wealth, love and happiness into your life.

Christopher

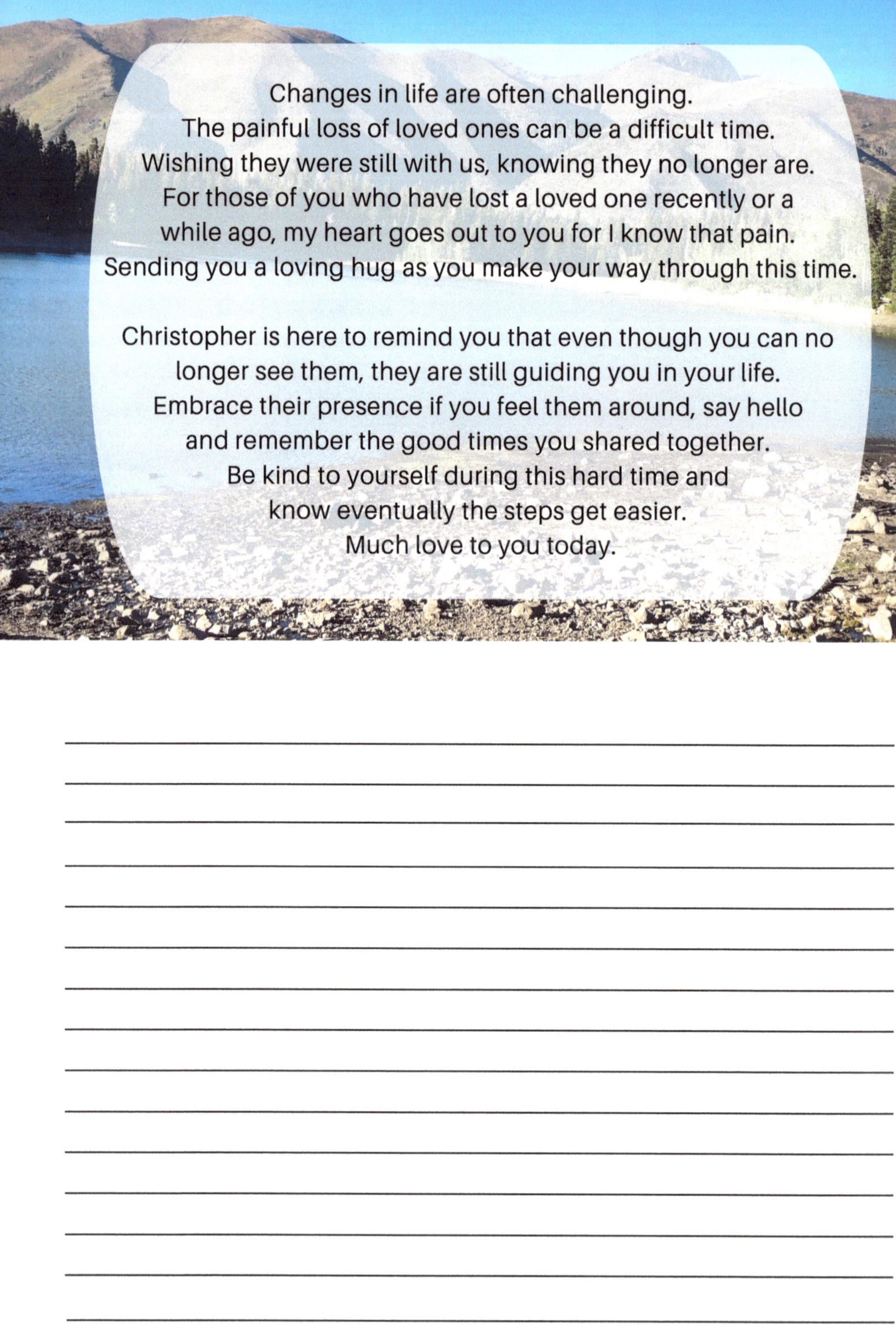

Changes in life are often challenging.
The painful loss of loved ones can be a difficult time.
Wishing they were still with us, knowing they no longer are.
For those of you who have lost a loved one recently or a
while ago, my heart goes out to you for I know that pain.
Sending you a loving hug as you make your way through this time.

Christopher is here to remind you that even though you can no
longer see them, they are still guiding you in your life.
Embrace their presence if you feel them around, say hello
and remember the good times you shared together.
Be kind to yourself during this hard time and
know eventually the steps get easier.
Much love to you today.

Are you ready to step into a new chapter? Are you still grieving?
There is no time frame on moving forward.
What is a favorite memory you shared with your loved one?
May peace fill your heart and your light shine again.

May positive affirmations and sayings
of gratitude continue in your life.
You deserve an abundance of love and laughter.

I am overjoyed you found this journal.
Thank you for your happiness and the light
that shines for yourself and others.
I am honored to have been able to walk this journey with you.
May love, light, happiness and freedom be with you always.

Artist's Story

Adventures of Celerina started with the desire to eat mostly fresh
fruits and vegetables. Celery quickly became a favorite vegetable.
My friend was surprised how much celery I ate in a day and after our
conversation on its health benefits, the nickname Celerina came to be.

Fast forward a year and 1/2 later, I decided to retire from my 20
year hairstyling career where I worked with some amazing people.
Their friendship, love and support brought a great deal
of encouragement to my life.

When I no longer had the responsibility of being a business owner,
things seemed to fall into place. I found renters for my house,
I had money to travel to most of the places I'd always wanted to see.
I packed up my Toyota 4runner, loaded up my dog and hit the road.
Living my dream.

The trip was hard, rewarding, freeing, eye opening, inspiring
and set me on a new creative journey.
Reviewing my trip pictures and remembering all the
wonderful people I was blessed to work with in the past,
I began combining them together into intuitive drawings.

I want to remind others the way we believe shapes our
present and future. There is an amazing world
out there filled with experiences worth doing if you desire.

This journal was created to inspire you to explore; to discover the
internal beauty of yourself and the beauty that surrounds you.

Myriah

Thank you